GROWTH MINDSET JOURNAL FOR BOYS

This book is dedicated to

. . . .

WRITE YOUR NAME HERE

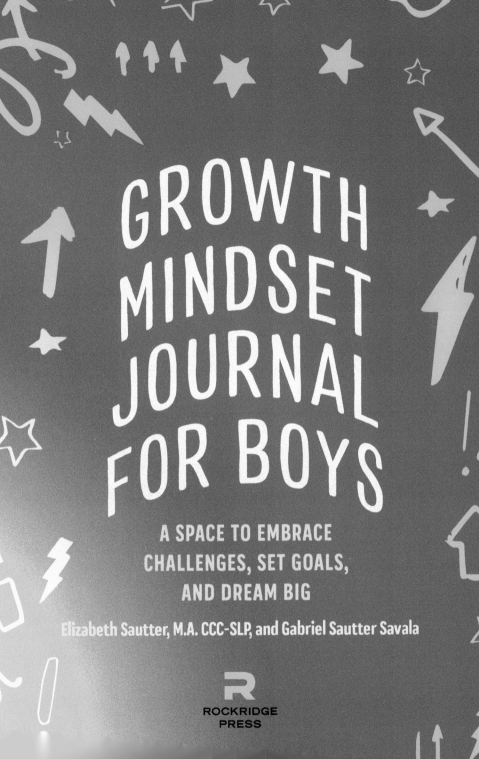

GROWTH MINDSET JOURNAL FOR BOYS

A SPACE TO EMBRACE CHALLENGES, SET GOALS, AND DREAM BIG

Elizabeth Sautter, M.A. CCC-SLP, and Gabriel Sautter Savala

R

ROCKRIDGE
PRESS

For general information on our other products and services or to obtain technical support, please contact our Customer Care Department within the United States at (866) 744-2665, or outside the United States at (510) 253-0500.

Rockridge Press publishes its books in a variety of electronic and print formats. Some content that appears in print may not be available in electronic books, and vice versa.

TRADEMARKS: Rockridge Press and the Rockridge Press logo are trademarks or registered trademarks of Callisto Media Inc. and/or its affiliates, in the United States and other countries, and may not be used without written permission. All other trademarks are the property of their respective owners. Rockridge Press is not associated with any product or vendor mentioned in this book.

Interior and Cover Designer: Emma Hall
Art Producer: Janice Ackerman
Editor: Mary Colgan
Production Editor: Matt Burnett
Production Manager: Michael Kay
Illustration: Courtesy of Shutterstock

ISBN: Print 978-1-64876-989-4
eBook 978-1-64876-990-0

R0

CONTENTS

WELCOME TO YOUR JOURNAL

You are about to go on an adventure to explore someone amazing, unique, and incredible: YOU! I have two sons who are working on their growth mindset, just like you are. Gabriel, who helped write this journal, often gets caught up in fixed-mindset traps. He wanted to practice having a healthier mindset and wanted to help you create one, too. Just like Gabriel, you can become stronger, braver, and happier just by changing the way you think. You can discover your dreams and how to make them come true. This journal can help you become your very best self!

let's go!

What Is Growth Mindset?

Your mind is what you think with, but your mindset is how you see things. It tells you if you can or can't do something. The best thing about a mindset is that you have the power to make it stronger and more positive. The first step is becoming aware of your own mindset.

A growth mindset is the belief that you can improve your ability to achieve your goals by building on your strengths and putting in effort and hard work. Do you remember when you first learned to read, ride a bike, or play a sport? Because you gave it a try, practiced, and worked hard, you had a growth mindset.

A fixed mindset is when you believe that you are born a certain way and that you can't ever change. This can make you feel stuck and frustrated. Maybe you thought, "I'm not good at this, so I'm going to give up." That is a fixed mindset taking over your thoughts. You can have a growth mindset in one situation and a fixed mindset in another or even fall in the middle. Try not to judge yourself or others for whatever kind of mindset you or they have. The important thing is to be aware of it.

In this journal, you will learn strategies to help you be your most awesome self. As you read and write in the following pages, think about the eight principles of a growth mindset:

1. Effort and hard work, not just talent, are the keys to success.

2. Mistakes and failures help you learn.

3. Unhelpful thoughts limit you.

4. You can create positive thoughts.

5. Frustration is a normal part of growth.

6. Comparison can hold you back.

7. Feedback and criticism are important for change.

8. Change is good!

This journal will help you know your strengths and explore how to meet your goals so you can feel more confident, brave, and happy. Anyone can build a stronger growth mindset, but you have to work at it. Are you ready?

How to Use This Journal

This journal is for you. If you want to share it with someone, like a friend or a family member, you certainly can! You can even ask for help if you want to. But you can also keep this journal private. There are no rules.

This book is full of activities and exercises. It helps if you do them in order because the exercises are designed like steps that will help you gradually build an awesome growth mindset.

Maybe you can make a home for your journal in a drawer or special place so you always know where it is and remember to use it. You can write in it each morning, or at night in a comfy spot with some music on. However you choose to use it, make this personal time part of your daily routine.

Don't worry about your handwriting or spelling because no one will grade this journal. It's for your eyes only! You can doodle and have fun with the drawing prompts. Use the quotes, goals, and challenges to inspire you.

This journal is designed to help you think about important stuff, like how to improve your self-esteem and get better at the things you like. Congratulations on opening this journal and getting ready to go, go . . . grow! Let's get started!

Let Your Strengths Shine!

Your brain is always busy. It controls everything you do, everything you feel, and the things you think and dream about. Your brain even changes and grows! During the first few years of your life, your brain grew really fast! It was learning new things about the world so you could become more independent.

You have your brain to thank for learning to walk, talk, eat, read, and maybe even ride a bike. But did you know that you can make your brain more powerful? If you pay attention to the world around you and the world inside you (your thoughts and feelings), you can use what you notice to become more aware and in control.

You can play sports or go to the gym to work out the muscles in your body, but how do you make your brain stronger? With brain exercise! Solving math problems, exploring nature, and learning to play an instrument are all exercise for your brain. Sometimes these "brain workouts" are pretty easy, while some might feel really hard. Let's start by thinking about the people and things around us that can help us work toward our goals!

Mindfulness

One way you can help your mind get stronger is by teaching it to pay attention to your body and to all the sights, sounds, and things going on around you. This is called *mindfulness*. Mindfulness is a powerful tool and can actually change your brain. It takes practice, but it's an important part of building a growth mindset.

Using your senses is a simple and fun way to practice mindfulness. To get started, close your eyes and listen to the sounds around you. Write down three things that you can hear right now.

1. ....

2. ....

3. ....

Open your eyes and look around you. Write down three things you see.

1. ....

2. ....

3. ....

Close your eyes again and notice what you can feel. Can you feel the chair or bed you're sitting on? How about the clothes on your body or the hair on your head? List three things you can feel right now.

1. ....

2. ....

3. ....

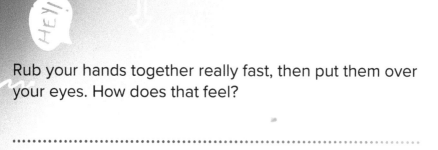

Rub your hands together really fast, then put them over your eyes. How does that feel?

∙∙

What sensations can you feel in the rest of your body? Are you hot, cold, or just the right temperature? Can you feel your heart beating? Can you feel your breathing? Take a minute to notice all the sensations and then write them on or around the figure.

Pick one of those sensations and write about what you think is causing it. For example, if your eyes feel heavy, maybe you are tired.

∙∙

∙∙

∙∙

What's on your mind today? What do you start thinking about when your thoughts drift away from this journal?

....

....

....

Imagine that you pressed a PAUSE button and froze the whole world. How would you feel in that silent stillness?

....

....

....

Circle any feelings you have right now.

Strong   Worried   Happy

Focused   Brave   Angry   Proud

Inspired   Scared   Tired

Sad   Embarrassed   Calm

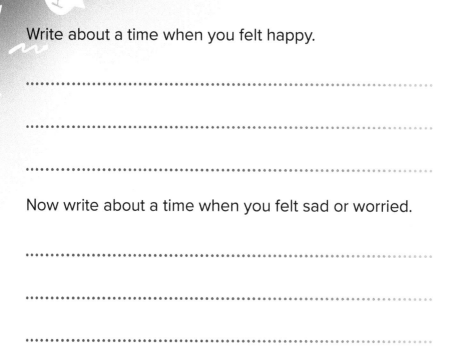

Write about a time when you felt happy.

· ·

· ·

· ·

Now write about a time when you felt sad or worried.

· ·

· ·

· ·

> "What day is it?" asked Pooh.
> "It's today," squeaked Piglet.
> "My favorite day," said Pooh.
>
> —A. A. Milne

Me, Myself, and My Strengths

"Getting to know yourself" might seem like a strange concept. After all, who do you know better than *you*? People tend to focus on what they wish they could change about themselves, and not on how great they already are. Knowing your strengths is an important part of a growth mindset. You can think of these strengths as your superpowers!

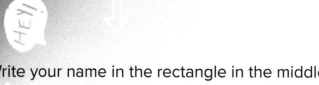

Write your name in the rectangle in the middle. Then fill in the squares with things about you—like the people in your life and what you like to do.

THINGS ABOUT ME

YOUR NAME HERE

List three of your strengths, like drawing, being a good listener, or telling jokes.

....

....

....

Choose one of those strengths. How did you develop it? Did anyone help you?

....

....

....

"We all have different gifts, so we all have different ways of saying to the world who we are."

—Mister Rogers

Trace your hand here. Write one thing you like about yourself on each finger. Do you notice any strengths you didn't think of before?

Another way to learn your strengths is to notice what makes you feel good. Write about the top three things you like to . . .

Think about:

....

....

Talk about:

....

....

Learn about:

....

....

Spend time doing:

....

....

Do you see any new strengths on these lists? Did anything show up on all four?

....

....

Caring for Your Brain and Body

Fun fact: Your brain is packed with 86 billion tiny cells called neurons. They connect to one another to build new pathways and pass on information. Like your body, your brain needs nutritious food, water, and rest. It also needs things like exercise, play, and connections with other people. If your brain and your body don't get these things, they won't work as well. Keep going to learn how to build *healthy habits* like eating nutritious food and getting plenty of sleep.

Eating is a healthy habit that can be part of a growth mindset! Next time you have a snack or a meal, take your time with it. Think about what it feels like, smells like, and tastes like. What is your favorite food? How would you describe it?

....

....

Drinking plenty of water is another healthy habit. It can keep your mind and body feeling good. Try drinking a glass—or even just half a glass—of water now. How do you feel different after drinking it?

....

Sleep is a healthy habit too. Do you feel rested most days? Here are some ideas about how to sleep more soundly. Circle the ones you'd like to try.

Turn off electronics an hour before bedtime.

Go to bed at the same time every night.

Don't have electronics in bed.

Make sure your room is completely dark.

Focus on your breathing before you go to bed.

Find the "just right" amount of:

Blankets

Darkness

Background noise

Even if you don't play a sport, you can get exercise every day. Take a few minutes to exercise now. You can jump rope, do jumping jacks, dance to music, or just run around the yard. How do you feel afterward? Do you have more or less energy?

....

....

....

Having emotional connections with other people is good for your brain, too. Think about someone you feel close to. How do you feel after hanging out with them?

....

....

....

Pick one of these healthy habits that you'd like to improve this week: eating, drinking water, sleeping, exercising, or connecting with others. How could you do that?

....

....

....

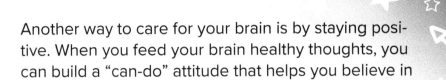

Another way to care for your brain is by staying positive. When you feed your brain healthy thoughts, you can build a "can-do" attitude that helps you believe in yourself. Cheer yourself on by finishing these thoughts.

I am proud of myself for...

....

My friends and family appreciate me because ....

....

I help others by ....

....

People like to be around me because ....

....

> ## "Be yourself; everyone else is already taken."
> —Oscar Wilde

HEY!

Being creative also helps your brain stay healthy. You can celebrate your strengths—and your creativity—through art. Fill this star with doodles of all the things that make you the star that you are.

Pursue Your Passions

You are figuring out your strengths and what you need to keep building your brain. That's great! Now let's think about what you want to do with that amazing brain and those superpower strengths. It's time to set some goals!

You have already achieved lots of goals—even if you don't realize it. Fill in the shapes with things you have accomplished, like tying your shoes and writing your name.

Look how far you have already come!

Take a minute to think about your passions. You can look back at page 11 to remind yourself of things you like to talk about, think about, and spend your time doing. Write down one passion that is especially important to you.

....

Think of one supercool goal that you have for that interest. For example, if your passion is playing the piano, you might come up with a goal to learn how to play the theme song for *Star Wars*.

....

....

Let's call this your **PASSION PROJECT**.

Remembering why you want to achieve a goal will help you stay motivated and on track. Fill in the WHY exercise to remember your passion project WHY.

What I want to do: ....

How I will feel when I accomplish it: ....

YIPPEE, YES, YEAH, YAY! Pick a Y word to congratulate yourself:

....

HEY!

Who in your life supports you when you have a goal?
We'll call these people your support team. Write their
names here.

....

....

....

How can your support team help you with your passion
project?

....

....

....

....

Write a letter thanking your support team for all the
ways they help you.

....

....

....

....

Imagine yourself accomplishing your passion project. This is called *visualization*. Draw a picture of what you see.

Baby Steps

Every big dream takes a vision *and* a plan
with steps to get there! Without a plan, it's
hard to accomplish a goal. The goal can feel
so big that you don't know where to start.
You might think the goal is impossible.
But if you break it into baby steps, you'll
see that by taking one step at a time,
you'll make the impossible POSSIBLE.

Describe a big goal of yours that might take a month or more to accomplish. This can be the passion project you wrote about or something different.

....

....

....

You might know more about how to achieve this goal than you think! Take a few minutes to write down everything you already know. What items do you need? Can you think of anyone who can help you? Do you know someone who has achieved this goal before?

....

....

....

....

....

....

....

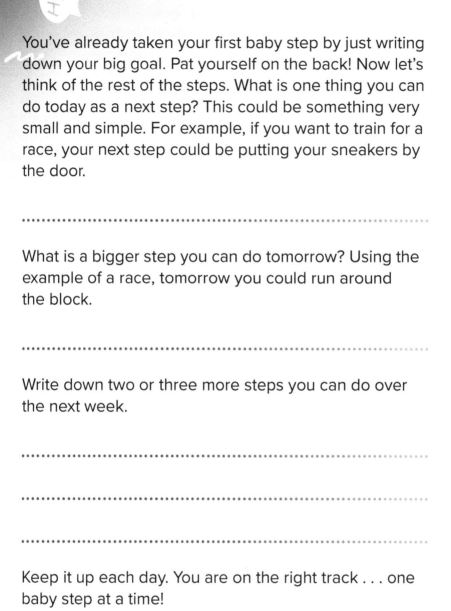

You've already taken your first baby step by just writing down your big goal. Pat yourself on the back! Now let's think of the rest of the steps. What is one thing you can do today as a next step? This could be something very small and simple. For example, if you want to train for a race, your next step could be putting your sneakers by the door.

....

What is a bigger step you can do tomorrow? Using the example of a race, tomorrow you could run around the block.

....

Write down two or three more steps you can do over the next week.

....

....

....

Keep it up each day. You are on the right track . . . one baby step at a time!

> # "A goal without a plan is just a wish."
>
> —Antoine de Saint-Exupéry

One important part of a growth mindset is being able to look in your own rearview mirror and learn from things you've already done. Write about a goal you achieved in the past.

....

....

....

How were you able to do it? Did anyone help you? Which superpower strengths did you use?

....

....

....

Did you learn anything that can help you with your new goals?

....

....

Think of something you've done that just didn't turn out the way you wanted it to. Why do you think it didn't work out?

··

··

What would you do differently if you tried again?

··

··

Did you learn anything that you can use for your new goal?

··

··

"Believe you can, then you will."
—Mulan

CHALLENGE YOURSELF!

Try to do a body scan a few times this week. Here's how!

Sit in a comfortable place or lie down. Close your eyes.

Scan your body with your mind to find any tight or uncomfortable feelings. Start with your feet. Then focus on your legs. Are they tight? If so, take a deep breath and try to relax them. Move to your belly. Take a deep breath in and then let it out. How does that feel? Now concentrate on your back and shoulders. Next, your arms and hands. Any tension there? Try to make them relax. Now move to your head, face, and mouth. Breathe in through your nose and out your mouth as many times as it takes to let all the tension out of your body.

This is called a body scan, and you can do this whenever you want or need to.

CHALLENGE YOURSELF!

Rate your healthy habits from 1 to 5
(1 being poor and 5 being great).

1. I eat healthy food every day.

   1   2   3   4   5

2. I drink six to eight glasses of water
   every day.

   1   2   3   4   5

3. I get enough sleep to feel rested.

   1   2   3   4   5

4. I exercise and move my body daily.

   1   2   3   4   5

5. I play every day.

   1   2   3   4   5

6. I connect with people every day.

   1   2   3   4   5

Put a star next to one healthy habit that
you want to improve.

CHALLENGE YOURSELF!

Try this magic trick!

1. Think about something that makes you angry, or a time when you felt angry, in the past. Does this make you feel angry now?

2. Now think about something that makes you happy or excited, or a time when you felt like that. Do you feel happy right now, just thinking about it?

Wow, you were able to change the way you feel all by yourself—just by controlling your thoughts!

Now that you know how, try this exercise one time this week when you are feeling frustrated, upset, or uncomfortable. Can you change your thoughts to make yourself feel better just like you did right now?

CHALLENGE YOURSELF!

Thank the people you're grateful to.
(Don't forget about yourself!)

Thank you, ..., for
                      (Write a name here.)

helping me ....

........................., I appreciate you
(Write a name here.)

supporting me in my healthy habits.

I'm proud of myself for working

hard at ....

Let's Celebrate!

Give yourself a pat on the back, a high five, or a hug for starting this journal and learning how to:

Be aware of your body, feelings, and emotions.

Identify your strengths and the people who can support you.

Take care of your body and brain.

Come up with a new project that excites you.

Set a goal and take baby steps to achieve it.

Your space to doodle and draw!

Being Brave

Being brave doesn't always mean being powerful or self-confident. When you see other people doing things that seem brave, you may think they are fearless. But the truth is that everyone is afraid sometimes.

Being afraid can even help you. Sometimes fear warns you that something is dangerous. It lets you know when to say no. Another time you may feel fear is when you are facing a challenge. You can let it stop you, or you can say, "Bring it on!" and find the courage to keep going. You can turn your fear into courage. Isn't that cool? Let's find out how!

Confronting Challenges

A challenge is something that requires
effort to complete. Some challenges are
given to you—like doing your homework
or cleaning your room. Others you might
set for yourself—like learning to juggle
or finishing a 1,000-piece jigsaw puzzle.
Challenges make your brain stronger.

Write about a challenge you're facing this week.

··

··

··

··

Close your eyes and take a mindful moment to notice your thoughts and feelings when you think about this challenge.

··

··

··

··

Be your own coach! What could you say to yourself to help you get started?

··

··

··

What's one baby step you could take to confront this challenge?

....

....

....

Have you faced a challenge like this before? What did you do then that could help you now? Include the people who could help you.

....

....

....

> "I think sometimes in life the biggest challenges end up being the best things that happen in your life."
>
> —Tom Brady

Challenges can be fun! Think of a fun challenge you can try this week. Maybe you want to build a toy boat that floats, or design your own board game. What do you need to do to prepare for this challenge?

....

....

....

....

Which parts of this challenge feel the most challenging?

....

....

....

Confronting challenges often means overcoming obstacles, which are things that stand in your way. What will you do if you hit an obstacle, like if you don't have a material you need?

....

....

....

Have you ever done an obstacle course? It's a challenging race with lots of obstacles to jump over, crawl under, or climb out of. Design your own obstacle course in the box!

Taking Risks

What do trying out for a play, tasting new foods, and making a new friend all have in common? They are all *healthy* risks that can make your life more fun, interesting, or meaningful. To take a risk means to do something even if you are not sure how it will turn out. Some risks are dangerous and should never be tried—like not wearing your seat belt. Other risks help you learn and grow by trying new things.

HEY!

When you are in your comfort zone, you are comfortable and relaxed, and you know just what to expect. List three things that are in your comfort zone, like playing your favorite game.

1. ....

2. ....

3. ....

Taking healthy risks might take you out of your comfort zone from time to time. List three things that are outside your comfort zone, like speaking in front of the class.

1. ....

2. ....

3. ....

Can you think of anything positive that could come from getting out of your comfort zone?

....

....

....

Write about a time when you were willing to take a risk to do something you wanted to do.

....

....

....

....

How did you find the bravery to take the risk? Did anyone help you?

....

....

....

....

What did you learn that might help you take another risk in the future?

....

....

....

....

HEY!

What is something you really want to do that feels scary or risky?

....

Imagine achieving this goal and circle how you would feel. You can add other words, too.

Happy   Excited   Proud   Pumped

Energetic   Relieved   Content

Accomplished   Calm   Peaceful

....

Now draw a picture of yourself accomplishing this goal.

Sometimes you might avoid taking risks because you're afraid of what other people will think of you. Has that ever happened to you? Write about it.

· ·

· ·

· ·

When you see one of your friends or someone on TV take a healthy risk to do something brave, what do you think about them?

· ·

· ·

· ·

You can reprogram your brain! Write about a situation that might make you worried about what someone else thinks about you ("He will laugh at me!"). Then turn the situation into something positive or helpful, like "He will think I'm brave!"

· ·

· ·

· ·

Never Quit!

Persistence is when you stick with something and don't give up—even when something is hard. This is also known as *grit* or *perseverance*. You need grit to build your growth mindset because it's how you keep going when you want to quit.

Think about a time when you didn't give up and completed a challenge. What happened?

....

....

....

....

Did you ever want to quit? Why didn't you?

....

....

....

How did you use your grit to keep going? How did you feel when your challenge was complete?

....

....

....

....

Write about a time when you gave up on something.

....

....

....

....

....

....

....

....

Make a check mark next to the thoughts that got in the way of completing your goal.

☐ It felt too hard.

☐ I didn't want to fail.

☐ I was too stressed.

☐ I felt scared.

☐ It was boring.

☐ I was too tired.

☐ I felt like I couldn't do it.

☐ ....

☐ ....

Thoughts like those can stop you in your tracks. You can get around them by flipping a switch in your brain to think about it differently. Here are some things you can say to yourself when you get discouraged.

Check the ones that you think would help you most.

☐ This is hard, but I have what it takes to persist.

☐ I am growing and learning as I try.

☐ I can take a break or ask for help when I get stressed.

☐ When I try new things, my brain gets stronger.

☐ I am proud of myself for trying hard.

☐ It's okay to feel discouraged.

☐ Next time I try this, it will be easier.

What is something else you could say to yourself when you want to give up?

··

> "The most certain way to succeed is always to try just one more time."
>
> —Thomas Edison

HEY!

When you feel like giving up, think about how you want to feel tomorrow or next month. How can you be a go-getter instead of a give-upper?

....

....

....

Not giving up takes grit. Write about a character from a book, movie, or TV show who has grit.

....

....

....

Do you have anything in common with that character? What can you learn from them?

....

....

....

Positive Self-Talk

Thoughts are like little voices in your head that can be helpful, encouraging, and positive. But they can also be negative, sometimes, and make it hard for you to move forward. They talk so fast that it's hard to control them. Take a minute to slow down and pay attention to what your voice is saying.

Think about the little voice in your head that sometimes gets in your way. Let's call that voice your *invader*. Circle the statements that your invader says to you from time to time.

I can't do this.   This is boring.

I'm not good enough.   This isn't fair.

I'm not..........enough.   People will laugh at me.

What other things has your invader said to you?

....

....

....

> ## "May your choices reflect your hopes, not your fears."
> —Nelson Mandela

Did you know that your mind also has a protector? It's your *inner coach*, who cheers you on and keeps you going. Here are some things an inner coach might say:

I can do this.

I'm good at learning new things.

I'm proud of how hard I worked.

I am good enough.

People like me for who I am.

What other things might your inner coach say to you?

....

....

What does your inner coach look like? Draw them here!

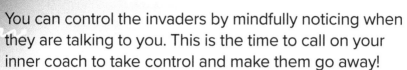

You can control the invaders by mindfully noticing when they are talking to you. This is the time to call on your inner coach to take control and make them go away!

Ask your inner coach to practice taking control of these negative thoughts right now. This is called positive self-talk. Here is an example of how it works:

Negative: I played poorly at my baseball game today.

Positive: I know I can play better in our next game if I practice this week.

Now it's your turn! Use your inner coach to write positive statements after each negative one.

Negative: This homework is too hard for me.

Positive: ....

Negative: Nobody wants to hang out with me.

Positive: ....

Negative: I'll never be as good as that guy at ....
Positive: ....

You can help your inner coach be more powerful by spending time thinking positive thoughts. Let's call this your positive thinking practice.

Three people who make you smile and feel loved:

1. ....

2. ....

3. ....

Three things that make you laugh or put you in a good mood:

1. ....

2. ....

3. ....

Three places that make you feel peaceful and happy:

1. ....

2. ....

3. ....

Your Growth Mindset Toolkit

Just like a carpenter fills a toolbox with a hammer, nails, and a screwdriver, you can fill your growth mindset toolbox with *brain tools*, or strategies, to help you in any situation.

We all need different tools in our toolbox for different situations. List the tools that you need to do your homework, like your schoolbooks or computer.

....

....

....

....

Not all tools are things you can touch. Brain tools are just as important. Check the strategies that you think might help you if you were having a hard time with your homework.

☐ Positive self-talk
☐ Taking a break
☐ Asking for help

☐ Trying a new approach
☐ Listening to music

Can you think of any others?

....

....

....

Have you heard the phrase "trial and error"? Sometimes the plans you make and the tools you use aren't the best match. Can you think of a time when you tried a strategy but it didn't work out?

....

....

....

When this happens, you may need a backup plan. That is when you go back to your toolbox and try something different. Set up a backup plan here for something you are having trouble with. Write the project or goal on the top line.

....

First, I will ....

But if it doesn't work, I will try ....

....

If that doesn't work, I can try ....

If that still doesn't work, I will try ....

....

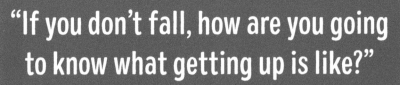

> ## "If you don't fall, how are you going to know what getting up is like?"
> —Stephen Curry

You can also use tools from your toolbox when you're feeling stressed or worried. Check the strategies that you think could help you when you're feeling anxious.

- ☐ Taking deep breaths
- ☐ Spending time doing something fun
- ☐ Exercising or taking a walk
- ☐ Talking with a friend
- ☐ Talking with your parents
- ☐ Writing in a journal

What are some other things that help you feel better when you're worried?

....

....

....

Write about a place that makes you feel calm.

....

....

CHALLENGE YOURSELF!

Design your toolbox! Draw a picture of a toolbox on a piece of paper. Make a list of all the tools inside the toolbox you think might help you when you are upset or stuck.

Post your toolbox on your desk or wall or put it in your binder to look at when you need to.

CHALLENGE YOURSELF!

Positive thinking can help you when you are upset, frustrated, sad, worried, or mad. It can also help you stay motivated and on track with your goals.

Color in these positive statements. As you color each one, repeat what it is saying in your head. Do you feel better after coloring them? Write your own positive statements in the empty bubbles and say them to yourself every day.

I have the tools and support that I need.

I can handle this!

Today is going to be a good day.

Learning new things is fun!

I am proud of my efforts.

I am a great person.

I choose to make today a great day.

CHALLENGE YOURSELF!

Find a jar or box and label it "I Am Grateful for My Growth Mindset." Place a notepad and pen next to it. Every night, take a minute to think about your day. Then write down one or two risks that you took, mistakes that you learned from, positive statements that you made, or things/people you are grateful for. Put the notes in the jar or box each night.

At the end of each week, take out your notes and read them to yourself or share them with someone.

CHALLENGE YOURSELF!

How comfortable are you with taking healthy risks? Look at the arrow and put an X where you think you fit.

I take a lot of
healthy risks.

I take healthy
risks sometimes.

I have never taken
a healthy risk.

Let's Celebrate!

Give yourself a thumbs-up and a big HOORAY for keeping up the hard work and learning how to:

Confront your challenges.

Take healthy risks and get out of your comfort zone.

Use positive self-talk and defeat your invaders.

Develop strategies to help you build a growth mindset.

Think positively to improve yourself.

"What you do makes a difference, and you have to decide what kind of difference you want to make."

—Jane Goodall

Your space to doodle and draw!

Discover What You Can Do

By now you realize that brains are awesome! You have been writing about some of the things your brain knows how to do and how to make it stronger. Just like a seed that needs water and nutrients to grow, your brain needs new experiences—and opportunities—to learn.

One of the best ways to grow your brain is by learning from mistakes. If you have always thought that mistakes are bad or embarrassing, it might seem odd to think of them as positive, but they are! Imagine if Michael Jordan missed a basket—and thought his mistake was so terrible he gave up playing basketball forever. Throughout his career, Michael saw those missed baskets as opportunities to learn and get better. That's part of what made him successful.

In this section, you are going to think about using your mistakes to build your brain. You can use your mistakes as brain exercises that can make new connections to help you get stronger, braver, and better at meeting your goals. You've got this! Let's talk about how to expect, inspect, and respect mistakes.

The Power of YET!

Learning new things takes time, but one word can make a huge difference: *YET*. It's not a magic word (you still have to do the work!), but it's one of the keys to building a growth mindset. Imagine you are challenged to run a race. You might want to say, "I can't run one mile without stopping." But what if you said, "I can't run one mile without stopping . . . yet!"? Do you see how the second statement changed your situation? With that sentence, you set yourself up to succeed!

Think of the last time you said you couldn't do something. Fill in the blank with what you said, and then read it out loud. How do you feel?

I can't ....

Now go back and write the word *yet* at the end of that sentence and read it out loud again. How do you feel now?

Fill in these three sentences with other things you can't do yet but would like to be able to.

I can't .... YET.

I can't .... YET.

I can't .... YET.

Voilà! You have three new goals.

> ## "I am always doing what I cannot do yet, in order to learn how to do it."
> —Vincent van Gogh

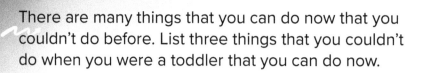

There are many things that you can do now that you couldn't do before. List three things that you couldn't do when you were a toddler that you can do now.

1. ....

2. ....

3. ....

List three things that you couldn't do five years ago that you can do now.

1. ....

2. ....

3. ....

Can you think of something you couldn't do just a month ago?

....

Have you ever felt like you couldn't do something because you don't have the skills or talent? For example, maybe you don't feel athletic or have trouble singing in tune.

....

....

Do you think you could like an activity even if you're not one of the best at it? Write about a time you had fun doing something you didn't think you were good at.

....

....

....

How did you feel afterward? Did you want to try again?

....

....

Think of something new and fun to learn, like roller-blading. You don't know how to do it . . . *YET*. What would you like to learn?

....

You can be your own T.E.A.M. when you learn something new. You just need Tools, Effort, Attempts, and Mistakes.

Tools: What tools do you need to get started learning your new skill?

....

Effort: How much effort will it take: a little, some, or a lot?

....

Attempts: How many attempts do you think it will take for you to improve the skill?

....

Mistakes: How will you learn from your mistakes?

....

Picture yourself in the future when you accomplish this goal. How will you feel?

....

....

Mistakes Are Opportunities

Mistakes are things that didn't go as planned. But mistakes aren't bad. Everyone makes them! If you pause to think about your mistakes, you can see them as gifts and opportunities to learn and grow. Let's unpack these gifts with an open mind.

Write about a mistake that you have seen someone else make.

....

....

Why do you think they made the mistake?

....

....

....

What do you think they learned from it?

....

....

....

Did you learn something too?

....

....

Not only are mistakes good for you, they're good for the world! Some really cool things were actually created by mistake, like light bulbs, the Slinky, and chocolate-chip cookies! Can you imagine another food that could be created by mistake? Draw it here!

Can you think of a mistake that you or someone else made that you were happy about afterward?

· ·

· ·

Do your mistakes ever make you laugh? How do you feel when you laugh instead of getting upset?

....

....

....

> ## "If you're making mistakes, it means you're out there doing something."
>
> —Neil Gaiman

One way to turn mistakes into learning opportunities is to figure out what went wrong and how you could do things differently next time. This is what scientists do all day long. Think about a mistake you made in the past. Can you act like a scientist and figure out what caused the mistake?

....

....

....

What did you learn from the mistake?

....

....

....

What can you do differently next time?

....

....

....

Sometimes people feel embarrassed when they make a mistake and don't want to admit they made one. Have you ever not wanted to admit to a mistake? How did that feel?

....

....

....

Write about a time that you admitted to a mistake. Did that feel different?

....

....

....

How can you help others learn from their mistakes? What do you usually say when someone makes a mistake?

....

....

....

Problem-Solving

Problems can bring on big emotions that might make you feel frustrated. If you let your emotions take over, you might not think as clearly. It's hard to come up with new solutions when your brain isn't working at its best! Managing your emotions is the first step to being an effective problem-solver.

Write about a problem that made you feel frustrated. Try to remember how your mind and body felt.

....

....

....

How were you able to calm down?

....

....

....

Check the strategies that you think might help you stay calm enough to think clearly next time you feel frustrated.

☐ Ask for help.
☐ Take a break.
☐ Take a deep breath.

☐ Say to yourself, "It's okay that I'm frustrated."

Problem-solving isn't a one-size-fits-all experience. Different problems have different solutions. Sometimes you need to get creative to find what works. Imagine that the school project you have been working on has just fallen apart. How can you make it better? List as many solutions as you can think of.

....

....

....

....

....

....

Which one do you think would work best?

....

> "I have not failed. I have found 10,000 ways that won't work."
>
> —Thomas Edison

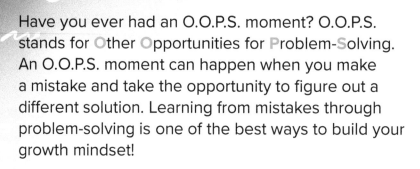

Have you ever had an O.O.P.S. moment? O.O.P.S. stands for Other Opportunities for Problem-Solving. An O.O.P.S. moment can happen when you make a mistake and take the opportunity to figure out a different solution. Learning from mistakes through problem-solving is one of the best ways to build your growth mindset!

Describe a time when a character in a book or movie made a mistake. What happened?

....

....

....

How did that character use this mistake and turn it into an O.O.P.S. moment by coming up with solutions?

....

....

....

Can you think of a different solution the character could have used?

....

....

Asking for help is another important problem-solving tool. It can be hard to ask for help, but like everything else, it gets easier with practice! There may be different people you go to for help with different situations. Who are some people you would go to for help with these problems?

School: ....

Friends: ....

Your health: ....

Your feelings: ....

Making decisions: ....

Do people come to you for help? Write about a time you helped someone else with a problem.

....

....

....

....

PLAY

My Flexible Brain

Your brain has the ability to stretch and expand, just like elastic! You might have heard the sayings "be flexible" or "go with the flow." When you are working with other people or trying to solve a problem, it helps to be flexible, but this takes practice!

Let's go!

What can you do with something that is flexible, like a rubber band, that you can't do with something stiff, like a stick?

....

....

How would your brain benefit from being more like a rubber band than a stick?

....

....

"Attitude is a little thing that makes a big difference."

—Winston Churchill

When your brain is flexible, it can help you see things in different ways.

Take a look at this image. What animal do you see? Now turn your head to the right and look at it sideways. Do you see a different animal now?

This image can look like either a duck or a rabbit. This is because there are multiple ways of seeing things.

Can you switch back and forth from seeing a duck or a rabbit? Look around you. Do you see anything that could be seen in more than one way?

Building a flexible brain will help you accept and deal with things that change every single day! List three things that can change daily, like the weather.

1. ....

2. ....

3. ....

Think of a time when you were not expecting something to change, but it did anyway. What happened? How did it make you feel?

....

....

Can you think of a time when something changed unexpectedly, but it turned out to be even better than you had imagined?

....

....

....

Life doesn't always go as planned. Sometimes you need a Plan B! Think about a Plan B for these situations.

Plan A: You planned to hang out with a friend, but they got sick and couldn't come over.

Plan B: ....

Plan A: You wanted cereal for breakfast, but there was no milk.

Plan B: ....

Plan A: A friend came over to watch a movie, but the Internet went out.

Plan B: ....

Plan A: You went to play basketball at the park, but it started to rain on the way there.

Plan B: ....

Getting Unstuck

The opposite of flexible thinking is *stuck thinking*. Sometimes stuck thinking happens when you are having trouble seeing things in a different way. Maybe you are dealing with a change, or maybe you feel worried about how something will turn out. Instead of going with the flow, you get stuck in the mud. Let's look at how you can get unstuck when this happens.

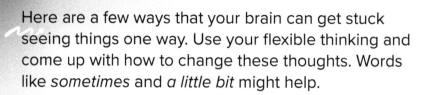

Here are a few ways that your brain can get stuck seeing things one way. Use your flexible thinking and come up with how to change these thoughts. Words like *sometimes* and *a little bit* might help.

Stuck Thinking: I am right. You are wrong.

Flexible Thinking: ....

Stuck Thinking: This is good. That is bad.

Flexible Thinking: ....

Stuck Thinking: I want all of that or nothing.

Flexible Thinking: ....

Stuck Thinking: Math is fun. Science is too hard.

Flexible Thinking: ....

Wanting things to be perfect can also make you get stuck. Let's look at the process, focus on the possibilities, and push "perfect" out of the way.

Describe a time that you wanted something to be perfect and it wasn't.

··

··

··

Practice imperfection! Stick a pencil between your toes and use your foot to draw a picture in the box. What's cool about your picture that wouldn't be true if it were perfect?

Write about a time when you were in a group and wanted to play something or do something one way, but everyone else wanted to do it another way.

· ·

· ·

· ·

How did you feel?

· ·

· ·

Did you find a way to go with the flow, or did you get stuck?

· ·

· ·

· ·

Getting stuck in the mud can hold you back and keep you from having fun! Sometimes it can help to just enjoy doing things without worrying how they will turn out.

Think about a school project that you are doing or have done recently. How can you shift your focus from the final outcome to enjoying the time you spend working on it?

....

....

....

What are some brain tools to help you go with the flow if you get stuck during your project?

....

....

....

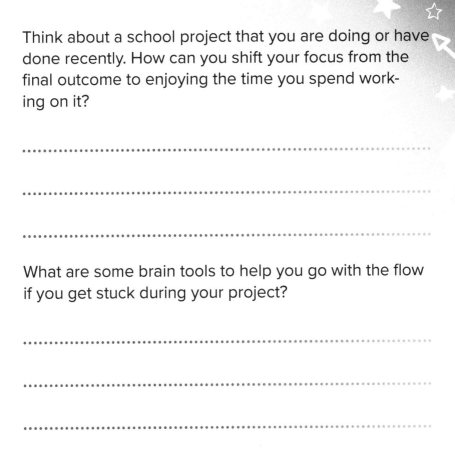

"If you look for perfection, you'll never be content."

—Leo Tolstoy

Seeing things in a different way can help us understand that mistakes aren't bad. Think of a mistake you might make, and then write about it from another point of view. For example, maybe you dropped your sandwich on the floor. Write a story about that from your dog's point of view!

CHALLENGE YOURSELF!

Do three things that usually feel easy and that you do perfectly. Now do those things a different or more difficult way so that they do not come out perfectly. For example, use your opposite hand to write your name or close your eyes and bounce a ball. Notice the thoughts and feelings you have. How can you be kind to yourself when doing things that are different and not perfect?

CHALLENGE YOURSELF!

Your brain is adapting to new situations every day—sometimes without realizing it. One example is when you are reading and you understand multiple meanings of words that are spelled the same!

Write down the different meanings of the following words:

Bat: ....
....

Watch: ....
....

Ring: ....
....

Mold: ....
....

Duck: ....
....

CHALLENGE YOURSELF!

We learned already that chocolate-chip cookies were made by mistake. If the baker had done things perfectly, we wouldn't have those delicious treats! Try putting together some favorite ingredients in a new way—maybe ice cream and watermelon, or bananas and potato chips. It won't be perfect, but it might be scrumptious.

Let's Celebrate!

Give yourself a round of applause! You have learned how to:

Change your mindset and your thoughts.

Embrace mistakes and learn how they can be helpful.

Be a problem-solver and ask for help.

Learn how to flex your brain and come up with different solutions.

Use strategies to remain calm.

"The privilege
of a lifetime
is being
who you are."

—Joseph Campbell

Your space to doodle and draw!

It Takes a Team

It is great that you are starting to know yourself better and feel good about the amazing person you are. Feeling good about yourself helps you have confidence when working with other people. It also helps you collaborate with them.

When you work with other people, they may give you input and tell you what they think and feel. This input is called *feedback*. It can come from a teacher, a coach, your family, or your friends. You can also give feedback to others. Learning how to listen to feedback is an important skill to practice, even though it can sometimes be hard. This is another way to have a growth mindset.

Like everything else, working with others takes practice. Let's start expanding this part of your growth mindset!

Be Yourself . . . You Are Awesome!

It's totally normal to sometimes feel like you are not good enough or worry about what other people think. When you become aware of these feelings, you can turn them around. Use the opportunity to learn new things from other people and grow by working together.

You have a lot to offer! Pretend someone wrote you an invitation to be a part of their group project and said why they chose you. What would it say?

....

....

....

....

What strengths can you contribute to the group?

....

....

....

....

Why do others like working with you?

....

....

....

....

When you are aware of how awesome you are, you can let that awesomeness shine! What strengths and talents do you feel comfortable showing other people?

....

....

....

What are some of your hidden strengths or talents that you don't share with people very often? For example, maybe you like to write stories, but you've never shown them to anyone.

....

....

Be a friend to yourself! What would you say or do to encourage yourself to share these hidden strengths with others?

....

....

It's okay not to tell everyone all your thoughts and feelings, but it's a healthy habit to share some of them with people you trust. Think about the thoughts and feelings that you don't share. Why do you keep them to yourself?

....

....

....

How do you think it might help to share some of these thoughts and feelings with others?

....

....

....

List the people who you might feel comfortable sharing these thoughts and feelings with.

....

....

....

....

HEY!

It's great to get along with people and hang out with your friends. Remember that it's also important to know what makes you happy and sometimes do your own thing! Describe a time when you did what your friends wanted to do but you really wanted to do something else.

....

....

....

Can you think of a time when you did your own thing, even though your friends did something different?

....

....

....

How did that make you feel?

....

....

....

Feedback Is Your Friend!

Just like food helps your body grow, feedback builds your growth mindset. You might not always like hearing about the things you can do better, but it is an important part of learning and maturing.

Feedback can cause many different feelings. Circle any words that describe how you have felt when someone gave you feedback.

Angry   **Sad**   **Embarrassed**   Happy

Grateful   **Frustrated**   Proud

Resentful   Inspired

Write about a time when someone gave you feedback that was really helpful.

....

....

....

Write a thank-you letter to that person here!

....

....

....

....

....

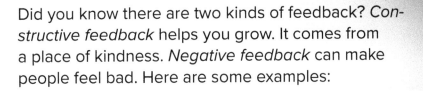

Did you know there are two kinds of feedback? *Constructive feedback* helps you grow. It comes from a place of kindness. *Negative feedback* can make people feel bad. Here are some examples:

Constructive feedback:

This cake is yummy. Have you tried it with chocolate chips?

I had fun hanging out. Next time, can you pass the ball to me more?

Negative feedback:

That's a horrible job. I could do it better.

You shouldn't have done it that way. What were you thinking?

Look at this list of feedback statements. Circle the ones that are positive and cross out the ones that are negative.

Your book report was boring.

I appreciate when you share with your sister.

You run funny.

Try swinging the tennis racket this way. You're almost there!

Even positive feedback isn't always easy to hear. Can you think of a time that you got feedback that could have helped you, but you didn't want to listen?

....

....

....

Can you use it now? Write down what you could do to learn and grow because of that feedback.

....

....

....

Have you ever given someone negative feedback? How could you have made it constructive feedback instead?

....

....

....

When someone gives you feedback, it's helpful to be humble and learn from what they are saying. You can be humble by not bragging or boasting and not taking all the credit for yourself. Who are some people who you admire for being humble?

....

....

....

Here are some statements that are not humble. Can you rewrite them to be humble?

We won the game because I scored three goals.

....

I'm the funniest person in my class.

....

She won the science fair this year, but I won it every other year.

....

Collaboration Is Cool

Collaboration is working with others toward a goal that each person can help with. You collaborate at home and at school, probably without always realizing it. Collaboration usually requires *compromise*. That means you find things you can all agree on, even if everyone doesn't get exactly what they want. Collaboration and compromise aren't always easy, but they can bring a lot of fun and growth into your life.

Write about a time when you worked or played with others recently.

....

....

....

....

....

What did you do to help the group or team?

....

....

....

....

....

....

....

Practice compromising! How would you compromise in these situations?

You want to play a board game with your friends, but they want to go to the park.

How would they feel if you told them they had to play the board game with you?

....

How can you compromise?

....

You want to play first base for the kickball game, but other kids do, too.

How would the team feel if you demanded to play first base?

....

How can you compromise?

....

You want to have some alone time, but your parents want to spend the day with you.

How would your parents feel if you refused to spend any time with them?

....

How can you compromise?

....

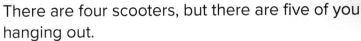

There are four scooters, but there are five of you hanging out.

How would the person without a scooter feel when the rest of you zoomed off?

....

How can you compromise?

....

"The best way to lift one's self up is to help someone else."

—Booker T. Washington

"You can go first." "Let's work together!" "What do you think?" These are all statements that a good collaborator might use. List some other things you could say.

···

···

···

What are other ways that you can help be a collaborator? (Hint: Your body language and actions also send messages.)

···

···

···

How do you feel when you are a good collaborator?

···

···

···

Draw a picture of things you like to do with other people.

Learning from Others

One of the best ways to learn new things and how to solve challenges is by watching other people. By paying attention, asking questions, and learning from their mistakes and successes, you can grow and learn, too!

It might be uncomfortable to ask for help, but with courage and practice, you can do it! Knowing when you need help and asking for it is called *self-advocacy*. Write about a time when you asked for help.

....

....

....

Can you think of a similar situation where you didn't ask for help?

....

....

....

Which one worked out better?

....

Did you know that you can also help others? Describe a time when you were able to help someone else and how it made you feel.

....

....

....

Asking others for help makes them feel useful. Here are some ways to ask people for help.

I like your writing style. Can you read this over before I turn it in?

I saw you skateboarding. Can you show me how to do that?

Can you think of others?

....

....

> "I think, 'Team first.' It allows me to succeed. It allows my team to succeed."
>
> —LeBron James

Imagine you are building a giant playhouse with a group of people. Every person is responsible for a different room. Draw a picture of your Dream Team— all the people with different skills who you would like for your team, like someone to help keep things organized and someone to choose all the colors. They can be real people, book or TV characters, or people from your imagination. Draw your playhouse, too!

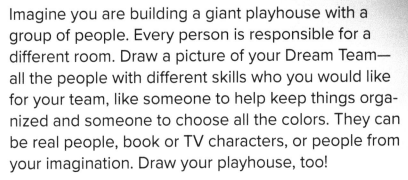

Conflicts happen when people disagree or have problems working together. Conflicts are a good way to practice learning from mistakes—either your own or someone else's. Write about a time when you had a conflict with someone on a team or in a group.

....

....

....

How did you handle the conflict? What did you learn from it?

....

....

....

Here are some healthy ways to handle conflicts. Circle the ones you might want to practice.

Listen to each other.

Step into the other person's shoes to see the situation from their perspective.

Talk it out.

Compromise.

Keep On Keeping On!

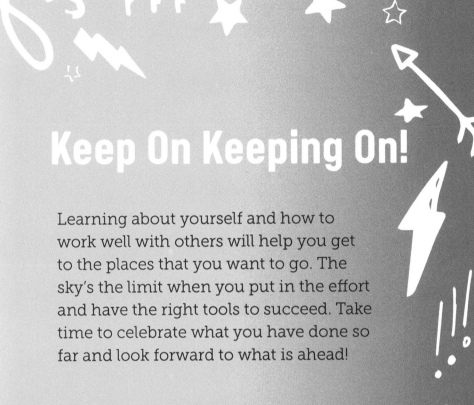

Learning about yourself and how to work well with others will help you get to the places that you want to go. The sky's the limit when you put in the effort and have the right tools to succeed. Take time to celebrate what you have done so far and look forward to what is ahead!

HEY!

List three small successes you had today, like finishing your homework.

· ·

· ·

· ·

List two medium successes you had this week, like learning something new at school or home.

· ·

· ·

List one big success you had this month, like getting cast in a play.

· ·

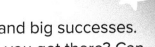

Reflect on your small, medium, and big successes.
What are the things that helped you get there? Can
you think of others? Add them to the list!

- ☐ Used positive self-talk
- ☐ Planned ahead
- ☐ Asked for help
- ☐ Collaborated with others
- ☐ Used your grit
- ☐ Took baby steps
- ☐ Took a healthy risk

☐ ....

☐ ....

☐ ....

☐ ....

> ## "It does not do to dwell on dreams and forget to live."
> —Albus Dumbledore

Picture yourself in the future meeting your goals and feeling happy and proud of your hard work. List three things that you can picture yourself doing in the near future, like reading a new book.

....

....

....

List three things you can picture yourself doing in the next year, like learning a new skill.

....

....

....

Draw how you will feel when you meet these goals!

Take some time to congratulate yourself and celebrate one little and one big accomplishment. You deserve it!

I am proud of myself for ....

because ....

I am proud of myself for ....

because ....

Having gratitude means being thankful for or appreciating the good stuff—and people—who support you.

List three things you are grateful for.

....

....

....

List three people you are grateful for.

....

....

....

CHALLENGE YOURSELF!

Write a simple poem about yourself that celebrates you!

The world knows that . . .

I am ....

I am ....

I am ....

The world doesn't know (yet) that . . .

I am ....

I am ....

I am ....

World, I am here, and I am great!

CHALLENGE YOURSELF!

Let's take a quiz. Circle true or false for each question.

1. It is important to give positive feedback. T F

2. I shouldn't bother people to ask for their help. T F

3. Being humble means I am a weak person. T F

4. My words and body language send messages to other people. T F

5. It's not okay to celebrate my accomplishments with others. T F

1.T, 2.F, 3.F, 4.T, 5.F

CHALLENGE YOURSELF!

Make a collage that shows all the cool things you have done with other people or would like to do with others. Use photos, magazine cuttings, drawings, or anything you can tape or glue to the page.

CHALLENGE YOURSELF!

When you started this journal, we talked about your big dreams. Now that you know more about how to help your brain learn and grow, think about your dreams. Draw a picture of your new and improved brain and fill it with your big dreams!

Let's Celebrate!

Give yourself a standing ovation! You have done great work learning:

About yourself and what makes you unique.

How feedback can help you learn and grow.

How to collaborate with and learn from others.

How to be proud of yourself and the amazing things you can do!

"It's not that I'm smart, it's just that I stay with problems longer."

—Albert Einstein

Your space to doodle and draw!

CONTINUE TO GROW!

Woo-hoo! Here you are at the end of this journal. It's almost like you had run a race and now you are crossing the finish line. Exercising your brain is just as impressive as exercising your body! How do you feel when you look back on all the thinking and writing that you have done? Maybe you learned some new things about yourself—and maybe you have even changed in some good ways. Sometimes it feels good to share those things with people who you care about. Remember, you can keep this journal private, but you can also share it with your friends or family.

Every day, try to think about the things you have learned. You can keep writing things down, too. Journaling is a good habit to have. Sometimes writing is a great way to think of questions, remember new information, or just talk to yourself about your thoughts. You can always come back and read what you wrote before. Doing this can help you remember things and give you ideas when you have new problems to solve or new things to overcome.

There will always be bumps and obstacles in your life. Everyone experiences those. When a person has a fixed mindset, it can be hard for them to overcome problems, but with a growth mindset, anything is possible. Changes in your thinking won't happen all at once. Sometimes you may get discouraged because you feel like you should know more than you do, and that's okay. Progress takes time, and each day is a new opportunity.

Every time you grow or learn or make some progress, pat yourself on the back for all the little steps you took along the way. Whether the steps you take are big or small, they are still wins! Remember, successful people have growth mindsets, and hopefully now you have one, too! Doing this much writing and learning and growing is something to be really proud of! Feel proud of the amazing person you are. Always have fun, keep smiling, and never forget that you are one awesome human being!

MORE SPACE TO WRITE AND DRAW

....

....

....

....

....

....

....

....

....

....

....

....

RESOURCES

Books for Kids

Beautiful Oops! by Barney Saltzberg

How to Be a Superhero Called Self-Control!: Super Powers to Help Younger Children to Regulate their Emotions and Senses by Lauren Brukner

A Little Spot of Confidence: A Story About Believing in Yourself by Diane Alber

Making a Splash by Carol E. Reiley

Mission: CONTROL!: A Big Feelings Adventure by Nan Arkwright

The Most Magnificent Thing by Ashley Spires

The Regulation Station by Leah Kuypers and Elizabeth Sautter

The Road to Regulation by Leah Kuypers and Elizabeth Sautter

Whole Body Listening Larry at Home! by Elizabeth Sautter and Kristen Wilson

Whole Body Listening Larry at School! by Elizabeth Sautter and Kristen Wilson

Your Fantastic Elastic Brain: Stretch It, Shape It by JoAnn Deak, Ph.D.

Books for Grown-Ups

Fall Down 7 Times, Get Up 8: Teaching Kids to Succeed by Debbie Silver

The Growth Mindset Playbook: A Teacher's Guild to Promoting Student Success by Annie Brock and Heather Hundley

Make Social and Emotional Learning Stick! by Elizabeth Sautter

Mindset: The New Psychology of Success by Carol S. Dweck, Ph.D.

Acknowledgments

Thank you to Mary Colgan and the Callisto team for providing this opportunity and guiding Gabe and me along the way.

To Ruth: I'm grateful for your magic; you make everything easier and better!

To Anthony: You keep everything going when these projects take over, and reminded Gabe and me how to use our tools when collaboration wasn't always easy. ☺

Julian, Gabe wants you to know that you are the best big brother ever!

About the Authors

ELIZABETH SAUTTER, M.A. CCC-SLP, loves to learn, grow, and gather amazing bits of research from her field of speech pathology to share with others. Elizabeth is a speech and language pathologist, and her passion for social-emotional learning led her to cofound Communication Works (CWTherapy.com), a multidisciplinary center known for all-ages individual and group therapy and school-wide services. She developed the book *Make Social and Emotional Learning Stick!* as well as books, decks, and other resources for kids and adults. She provides online trainings and also travels around the United States and Canada to provide presentations on social-emotional learning and building a growth mindset.

GABRIEL SAUTTER SAVALA, one of Elizabeth's sons, was excited to coauthor this journal and share his insights from a boy's perspective and what he has learned from building his own growth mindset. This process has helped him grow even more, just as he hopes it will help other boys like him. Gabriel is a middle school student who loves cats, playing chess, watching sports, cooking, and working on his own business, Gabe's Granola.

Elizabeth and Gabe live in Northern California with Julian (funny and loving older son/brother), Anthony (supportive and devoted husband and father), Mia (sassy, orange, and cuddly cat), and Lucy (sweet and lazy dog).

CPSIA information can be obtained
at www.ICGtesting.com
Printed in the USA
JSHW020743301021
20002JS00002B/2